The Canon of
THE
LONE
RANGER

The Canon of
THE LONE RANGER

Steve Goldman, in *Lone Ranger,* assures us once again that poetry has no parameters, boundless and free as the human spirit. I marvel at the volatility and resonance of language in *Lone Ranger,* a fusion of complex structures performed on separate levels, masterful antic inventions, street-smart rhythms. *Lone Ranger* is sure to become a collector's imperative, so get your signed copy at Steve's next appearance. This is what poetry's all about.

Ray Clark Dickson

Goldman's art has brought new life and a credibility to that uniquely American folk hero we know as The Lone Ranger whose adventures into the New World abyss are guided by a talking horse (Silver,) a side-kick (Tonto,) a dysfunctional family, a love life and enough doubts to keep the Freud in the narrative busier than ever. The reader is rewarded with an epic filled (with) good poetry and much insight.

Si Perchik

I could feel that this was very big, and see it becoming a real part of the canon of poetry in the next fifteen or twenty years...—it is a very considerable piece of work. You pull together times and places, feelings and resolutions, for yourself and for us, it's really wonderful. Sometimes we look out at the sunlight, and sense and enter into a kind of eternity. We contemplate that eternity, which work such as yours helps us to enter more completely or more often. This work does stand and live.

Lee Brunckhorst

I've read *The Canon of the Lone Ranger* with great pleasure. I'm impressed with the intensity of the work, all the way through. The very American conflicts in the poem move me—the shadow side of our hero worship. The Lone Ranger's woes are ones we all understand: family pain; the madness of war; the need to maintain an invincible image; a seemingly incurable loneliness that runs through the American psyche...and the mother wound of this country—not a simple issue, but a vitally important one. So, Thank You—for the deep seriousness of your work but also for the humor in it, which saves it from pompousness.

Holly Prado

The Canon of
THE LONE RANGER
A Hymn in Dysfunction
An American Life
and
The Autobiography of Just About Everybody

By Steve Goldman

Mor-Mun Press

©2011 by Steve Goldman

Illustrations by Dick Glass

All rights reserved. No part of this book can be reproduced without the express written permission of the author, except in the case of written reviews.

ISBN 978-0615591391

Revised Edition

MOR-MUN PRESS
11842 Venice Boulevard, Apt. D
Los Angeles, CA 90066
elkingo2.steve@gmail.com

Printed in the United States of America

Some of these poems were previously published in poeticdiversity.

Previously published by Sybaritic Press
www.sybpress.com

Acknowledgements

Song lyrics in "The Birth of The Lone Ranger"

"Gypsy woman tole mah mutha'..."
from the song *The Hoochie Koochie Man*
by **Muddy Waters**

"Meet de Boys on de Battlefront..."
from a 'war' chant *Meet the Boys on the Battlefront*
of the **Wild Tchoupitoula's**, a New Orleans
'black Indian tribe'—for Mardi Gras

Cover Design by **Dick Glass**

Chris Yeseta— Design, Layout and Prepress

RD Armstrong— "Rabbi"

Dedication

To every son of a bitch/daughter of a bastard and his or her memory, in and around Venice, CA from 1970 to date, who ever bought me a drink, stood me to a meal, gave me a day's work, lent me 10 bucks, laughed at my jokes, sighed at my poems, fenced with me, sang with me or took my weeping face on his or her shoulder. Y'all know who you are.

To "The Boys," notably Jimmy Gitter & Hank Crystal who respectively encouraged me to finish this and saw value in it.

To the memories of the late Joanne Nilan and the late Annette LeBleu, mothers and poets both, who shed great light on the matters of motherhood and mothers and sons.

The poem
"The Lone Ranger and His Mother: The Reconciliation"
is gratefully and specifically dedicated to Ioanna Warwick and David Oliveira, respectively its catalyst and "midwife."

Special thanks to Sandra Rader, Sharon Doubiago, Velene Campbell, and Marie Lecrivain, and Karin Spritzler: Consigliera.

And a special broad-spectrum thanks to Joan Pinkney.

"*The social order must be preserved,
yet paradoxically the freedom of the
individual may not be infringed.
I myself have always been alone.*"

**Occasional Remark By 'The Lone Ranger'
(from the poem "The Funeral of Steve Goldman"
by Steve Goldman—in The Lone Ranger's Voice)**

"A fiery horse with the speed of light,
A cloud of dust
And a hearty
'Hi Yo Silver: Awaaaaay!'"

From the Litany

Table of Contents

Prologue: The Lone Ranger Dines in Vienna… *1*

Part the First
The Birth of the Lone Ranger *4*
The Lone Ranger's Earlier Dating Practices *7*
The Lone Ranger's Boyhood: A Trinity *9*
Conclave *10*

Part the Second
The Lone Ranger Goes To War *14*
The Lone Ranger's Kid *16*
The Lone Ranger's Star *17*
Bro Ranger *18*
The End of the World: The Movie *23*
The Lone Ranger's Job Search *24*
The Lone In Ranger Old Age: Three Views #1 .... *25*
View #2 .... *27*
View #3 .... *28*
The Lone Ranger's Sister *30*
The Lone Ranger Finds True Love *31*
The Lone Ranger's Great Love Affair: The Aftermath *34*

Part the Third
The Quest for the Missing Mystic Mythic Father *40*
The Lone Ranger at the Moment of Death *57*
The Lone Ranger on Superman's Flight *58*
Dan Reid *60*
The Lone Ranger and His Mother:
    The Reconciliation *64*

Part the Fourth
Epilog *80*

Bio *83*

PROLOGUE:
THE LONE RANGER DINES IN VIENNA
WHILE SIGMUND FREUD HAS A BEER
IN TOMBSTONE, ARIZONA

The Lone Ranger,
mask, silver bullets, six-guns. Stetson and all
is dining alone in Vienna.
The place is small, inexpensive, out of the way
   and excellent.
He has had a classic wiener schnitzel with spatzele,
and a vegetable compote of some sort.
He has avoided wine.
He doesn't drink,
and besides, an exception would slow his
   lightening draw
although that is almost certainly academic here.

Now he is enjoying a black and bracing espresso,
and in a minute will light
a small Brazilian cigar;
a rarity for him.

The other diners
And the waiter
Are cutely curious at the apparition,
But never discourteous.

Outside, Silver drowses contentedly at the
   hitching post.
The Lone Ranger is contented too,
Feeling filled, serviced, expansive even
And gratefully less anxious than he does in
The West.

But he wonders:
"What the fuck
am I,
The Lone Ranger,
Doing In Vienna?"

By parity of reason
(by parody of reason)
Sigmund Freud,
alone,
has just entered a saloon
in Tombstone, Arizona.
The cowboys at the bar
gawk and taunt:
"Haw Haw. Lookit the greenie with the beard!"

Freud, unarmed, slight of stature, Jewish,
steeped in "Kultur und Gemutlichkeit,"
terrified of rowdiness and violence,
orders a beer,
sits at a table
and automatically camouflaged,
inwardly rages at the "goy animals".

A neurologist, alcohol calms, encourages and
   disinhibits him;
a mystic, it puts him limpidly in touch with
   mysteries and universals.
He produces and lights
a small Brazilian cigar,
virtually fixture with him
and wonders anxiously:
"Was I right to come here?"

These two are the same person,
epiphenomena of the deity Jesus,
who, as you know
is a black woman.

PART THE FIRST

THE BIRTH OF THE LONE RANGER

He is the proper firstborn son of a proper
New England couple,
born in Massachusetts before the Civil War—
the war that is fought in families:

His father a ship's chandler in that state,
his mother the scion of a great family I cannot
   name here.

It is the ideal wedding, and it is said of them
   that they actually resembled
the little statue figures atop the wedding cake.
The bells in the town's white steeple rang,
   proclaiming this.

But the father is haunted by demons of rage at
   his belittlement.
His older brother, Oliver Wendell Holmes, has
   overshadowed him
and he has no sanction, but only cold distance
   from his lordly parents
who favor the great judge.

His mother is enraged at the belittlement of her
   womanly lot.
Her whale-bone stayed corsets and bodices
   bind her in ways she is unable to know.

They are themselves children having children—
   do not want the child,
and have no way of knowing this.

But the baby is born with due pomp of
   announcement.

The firstborn, his is a bloody, long and painful
   birth.
His mother screams in murderously resentful
   labor for 36 hours,
in a time of primitive obstetrics.

Yet at the very moment of his birth, the Black
   slaves and the town's Indians,
seemingly in some kind of trance, chanted and
   bruited it among themselves:

>   "Gypsy woman tole' mah motha,
>   befoah Ah was born,
>   You got a manchile' comin', gon' be a
>   sonova gun!"
>   and
>   "Meet de boys at de battlefront,
>   Wild Tachapatoula gonna stomp
>   some rump!"

He is handsome and likely boy, cooing and
   puling in his cradle.

He will go to Harvard.

But when the pewter-plate moon rises over the flat hills of Massachusetts, and the witches of Puritanism ride, he is a were-baby, who dreams in his crib of black masks, white hats, silver guns, an Indian horseman silhouetted against an ochre Western moon, escape to the west on a Great White Motorcycle not even yet conceived, a fair young woman in gingham and bonnet spinning at her wheel, and of children and babies like himself everywhere.

His mother puts a coverlet over his cradle so, in her psychosis, she will not see him. There are holes in it, so the infant may barely breathe. But when that witches' moon rises over the Commonwealth, and plays through the window and onto the cradle, the shadow of the mask is already graven on the face of the neonate Lone Ranger, unbeknownst to his unknowing mother.

AN EXAMPLE OF THE LONE RANGER'S EARLIER DATING PRACTICES

The Lone Ranger has met a new lady, and doesn't *begin* to know how to handle it. "Play it by ear, Ace," says Silver. "Just take it one day at a time. If you fixate on either the past or the future too much, they're both traps. You could suffocate." They have been together so long, the horse talks to him.

Now Tonto appears. "Unnnggghhhhh: This is a fine howdyadoo Pal, after all we've been through! We've come a long way Baby, and because of you I've done just fine. But I'm not so lame as to suppose I can go it alone. You *are* the top banana. And we *can't* include *her* in our act!"

Now the Lone Ranger is in anguished consternation. Beads of sweat can be seen peeking from behind the black mask. He turns violently and shrieks the unthinkable: "Piss off you Injun' faggot!"

Now the lady in question herself enters.

"What's it gonna be, Dude? Relationship-wise, that is?" asks the woman/person/female/individual/human/entity whose name is Plain Jane Everygirl and who hails from the small town of Nextdoor, Texas. "Casual dating, exclusive dating, live together, marriage, can I sleep with other people, can you, do you want to? What's the story?" (Remember, this was back before AIDS, ed.) "You've heard of the proposed ERA Amendment, a body has a right to know, and what's more, I have my career to think of!"

Completely bonkers now, The Masked Man can only waffle and stammer: "Aww gawwwwwwwsh Jane, you sure are pretty."

"Flattering, Stud," says Jane, "but hardly relevant. May I have the envelope, please?"

Will the Lone Ranger resolve his ambivalence and confusion in the face of *this*, his greatest peril to date? What will be the fate of Plain Jane, and Silver, and Tonto? What of the long standing traditions of the past, and what does the future hold? To find out, be sure to tune in to the next thrill-packed episode as the Lone Ranger rides again in the *YES* bewildering days of the New West!

THE LONE RANGER'S BOYHOOD:
A TRINITY

The Lone Ranger played on the beach, the
    south 40, and the streets of the city
he romped in the surf, hunted varmints in the
    wooded border of the field, and played
punchball on the asphalt
he enjoyed none of it

his father was a boatwright, a farmer, an attorney
his father never took him to work
his mother fed him, fed him, and fed him

the other boys in the neighborhood snarled at him,
and girls were portrayed to him as Martians.

he grew up with ashes burning blind behind his eyes
already coalescing into the mask

CONCLAVE

Having just turned 45 years old,
The Lone Ranger's family has called a family conclave to discuss his
      Vocational Identity.
"Come in. Dear," says Mom Ranger.
"You boys look tired. Boys, how about something to eat, some
      nice pot roast?
Although I must say, Tonto, I never *could* understand what *you people* eat.
How 'bout a nice bison burger?"

"Uhhh, that's all right Mrs. Ranger," Tonto dissembles;
"We ate on the way over at a MacDona...uh...at the tribal headquarters cafeteria."

"Well Son," says Dad Ranger who is very old and puling in his beer. "Let's get to cases. We think it's high time you settled down and got a regular job, took off that mask, and got some responsibility. How 'bout it, Son?" (Dad Ranger says "How 'bout it. Son?" a lot.)

Now the LR's kid brother Kid Ranger, who is a Brilliant Young Attorney, holds forth. "You know, you're 45 years old now, and you still won't embrace reality. You persist in riding that stupid white horse, hanging around with this Indian faggot, and fighting crime and righting wrongs for no discernible income! No wife, no kids, no standing in the community! When the fuck are you going to *get with it?* I hate to say this, but the extremity of the situation and my deep concern for you, (singlely and severally speaking) leaves me no latitude. You always *were* and asshole, you *are* an asshole, and you'll *very likely remain one* unless you get a hold of yourself and shape up!!!"

Quick as a snake's tongue, and with *no conscious intent* on the part of the Lone Ranger, *both* deadly Colts flash up to bear, and, in percussive cacophony, the Brilliant Young Attorney perishes in a hail of silver bullets. This is signal, because the Lone Ranger has never before killed anyone.

"O you and your goddamn temper! Always you and your goddamn temper!" Pules Dad Ranger. "Are you never gonna straighten out? How 'bout it Son?!"

Mom Ranger is shrieking hysterically: "You got blood all over my broadloom! Clean it up this instant!" Slowly, inexorably, the Lone Ranger's misted eyes *and* the Colts begin to train on the aged parents, as Tonto, stepping into the line of fire says: "Uh, that's all right Mom, we'll clean it up tomorrow. We uh, really have to be going."

And gently but firmly pushing the Lone Ranger toward the door, he says to him: "C'mon John, we're late for our therapy group."

Part the Second

THE LONE RANGER GOES TO WAR

Lone Ranger or no, the Lone Ranger is drafted
    into the Army.
Because of his mythical, trans-temporal
    character, he serves simultaneously in
    WWI, WWII, Korea, Viet Nam and the
    Persian Gulf.
Forbidden his costume, mask and silver Colts,
he is issued a regulation uniform and weapon,
    and
denied his request to serve at his obvious
    military occupational specialty—
that of scout or sniper, employing his legendary
    marksmanship
        to shoot the guns from the enemy's
        hands, effectively but harmlessly.
There is no talk of that here. Here people get
    shot in the balls.

Being the Lone Ranger, he further requests that
    he be made
Commanding General, so he won't have to take
    any orders,
or the lowliest private so he won't have to give
    any.
Naturally, he is made a captain of infantry.

He strives to shield his men from the worst
    insane excesses of his superiors,
while obeying the orders of these superiors
    leavened by such reason as can be
    mustered in combat.

Being the Archetypal Loyal American, he
vigorously prosecutes
      The War Against the Enemy,
only now for once, he cannot adhere to his
prime value of never killing anyone.

Like so many who had gone before him, he
emerges from the war mad,
or at least greatly saddened for life.

THE LONE RANGER'S KID

The Lone Ranger meets his son,
estranged from him at birth.
A tall, handsome, lean and wiry kid of 21,
with that all too familiar resolute thrust of jaw.

"Hi Dad," says the Kid,
"Could I borrow Silver for tonight? I got a hot
　date with Pocahontas' daughter …"

*"Jesus Christ!" thinks the LR " lend him Silver?!!
I'm the Lone fucking Ranger!
And Silver is an essential part of being the
　Lone Ranger.
Without that big white nag, I'm nothin'!"*

"Uh whatsa' matter Son, can't arrange your
　own transportation?
　And are you sure this girl's right for you?"

"Don't give me racism. Dad, and as for Silver,
　　there are unimpeachable standards of
　　behavior and appearance which must be
　　kept!"

"Jesus" thinks the Lone Ranger, "this little
prick's altogether too much like me-
how could I possibly live with him?"

"And besides, he looks to be pretty fast
　with those hi-tech, double magazine, all-
　chrome 9mm automatics.

THE LONE RANGER'S STAR

The Lone Ranger is finally awarded a star on
   the Hollywood Walk of Fame.
It is the 1,848*th* such star ever awarded.
Wearing designer sunglasses in place of his
   mask—
now forbidden by the very law
he fought hundreds of years to uphold,
he is introduced by Sherman Bloch:
then Sheriff of L.A. County.
and his brother in law enforcement

The Lone Ranger, visibly pleased, smiles,
unveils the star
and, by way of acceptance and thanks intones:

"This star actually belongs to all of you -
my loyal fans who backed me and kept faith
   through all these long and lonely years
though at times the way was hard,
and to my dear, late friend Tonto,
supreme partner, exemplary human being,
(who rightly got his star here some years ago.)
I loved him very much."

"Hi Yo Silver. Awayyyyyyyyyyyyyyyyy!"

BRO RANGER

The Lone Ranger's secret older brother, Bro Ranger happens to ramble through town just by chance. He sits astride his once proud black stallion, now gone lank with age and nearly shot in the withers. Bro Ranger is himself past the doorstep of middle age, as his 4 day's growth of "pepper and salt" stubble shows. He is someone who over the years has been purged in the kiln of experience of all flux of frivolity, someone steeped by now entirely in the practical. His gear reflects this. He rides on a plain, brown, cowboy's working saddle and tack, creased and oily. He wears no ivory handled, match grade, silver chased Colts with an attendant firmament of silver bullets such as are hallmarks of the celebrity of his famous younger brother. Instead, a single worn, dull and undistinguished standard police model .38 Special in a tatty holster and rig rides his hip, and although the weapon is fully loaded, the slots on the cartridge belt are only intermittently and irregularly studded with bullets. His clothes stink from the trail. Still, notwithstanding his age and slight paunch, his calm level gaze and the relaxed thrust of his once finely modeled jaw, now gone slightly to flab, tell people of even the smallest degree of sensibility that this is one of the last persons you would ever want to trifle with.

Tying Old Black to the hitching post, he shambles into the Dusty Rose Saloon and Hotel, having in mind a quiet beer or 3 to slake the dust of the trail.

The Lone Ranger, having grown more sociable of late, is seated at a table in the back of the room, in a friendly card game with The Boys. Tonto, who does not play cards, is at his side. The brothers have not seen one another for better than 15 years, have lost track, and neither has any idea that there might be family in this town.

Bro Ranger has gone to an empty space at the bar near the entrance, and is on his first beer when, idly glancing around the room, his eyes happen to light on those of the Masked Man. And the moment is electric! Recognition is instant, mutual and simultaneous. There is a shocked hiatus.

The Lone Ranger is first to speak from under his rocketing eyebrows.

"You!" he expostulates.

"Howdy, Kid," says Bro.

LR: (agitated) "But, uh, you, I—you..."
Bro: "What can I say, Kid?"
LR: (quickly regaining some composure) "Uh, C'mere. C'mon over. Have a beer."
Bro: "Why shore."

Scanning the whole room which has now fallen watchfully silent, he ambles slowly over and sits down, placing *his own beer* on the table.

Bro: Howdy Tonto, Boys. (He knows of his brother's exploits and Tonto from the newspapers.)

Tonto: (confused) Unhhhhh...
LR: Uh well Bro. What's goin' on? I never heard.
Bro: (interrupting) Same old shit.
LR: Mom died and...
Bro. I know kid. I got a letter. I was in the war.
LR: You never came to the funeral.
Bro: I tol' ya Kid, I was in the Army.
LR: You could have written a letter.
Bro: Never was much of a hand at writin' an' besides Ah never did get along with Maw.
LR: You never did give a damn...
Bro: Uh well an' you were the apple of Mom's eye an' ya still would be if she was livin', what with yer pretty guns an' white horse an' all...

The chill at the table has grown palpable, as old inarticulate rages surface toward embodiment in irrelevant issues.

LR: And you? You're a drifter and a bum. What the hell good is that?

Both men are standing now, jaws canted forward.

Bro: Don't sass me Boy. I always *could* whip your ass!
LR: (with slow drawl, now over being nonplused, and fully the Lone Ranger again) Mebbe' so, stranger, but that was when we were kids. But now I'M THE LONE FUCKING RANGER!

Hands fibrilate above pistol butts, and the cowboys at the table scatter and dive for cover. After all, this is *the Lone Ranger* and his unheard of *Big Brother!* The moment is frozen, when, for the second time in Ranger family history, Tonto intercedes to avert mayhem. Thrusting the table aside and stepping directly into the line of fire, the prescient Red Man, holding restraining hands in both directions, says:—

Tonto: Unnhhh...it not good brothers fight. (beat) A scriptural referent might be 'It is not meet for brother to raise up hand against brother, but better to dwell in the same house in the fullness and righteousness of the land, in harmony therewith.' Uhhh.,, Proverbs 4:21 I think. (Remember, Tonto has been to Oxford on an Affirmative Action Scholarship.)

"Please, try to restrain yourselves, Kemo Sabiamous," he says, coining a Latinate pleural for the occasion.

Another frozen moment, then The LR and Bro are both seen slowly relenting. There is a beat: the moment is defused.

LR: (to Tonto)You are right, Kemo Sabe.
Bro: Wal, fuck it...

The hands float away from the handles of the pistols. There is another pause, a frozen, wooden pause.
Bro: So Boy, are you happy bein' a pretty-boy cop in all the newspapers and wearin' a mask an' no regular job an' no wife an kids...

LR: What would you know about wives and jobs an a coupla kids?
Bro: I had me a little spread up Kansas way after the war an' a little woman an' a couple of kids, an' the Injuns killed 'em and burned us out.
LR: (after looking imploringly at Tonto who shakes his head gravely) Oh. I'm sorry. I didn't know.
Bro: That's O.K. Kid, how could you know? But I asked you, are you happy doin' what you're doin'?
LR: No, but its all I know. I have to; I swore an oath.... Are you happy driftin' from job to job and having nothing but your freedom?-
Bro: No. Kid. Not happy. But I'm content. What more is there?
LR: Let's talk more at my camp outside of town. Let's save this for later.
Bro: Shore, Kid.

The cowboys are beginning to drift back to the tables, and the din of the saloon resumes. So let's leave them all there for right now. Perhaps the Masked Man and the Drifter will be able to continue talking.

THE END OF THE WORLD: THE MOVIE
(OR WHY MOVIES STINK)

Tonto is back from Oxford University
where he has just completed his doctoral degree.
He has been made
Regius Professor of Old West Studies
in Balliol College,
but now he is returning to duty with the Lone Ranger.

They pull up in a dusty draw near a ghost town.

"Looks deserted, Tonto," says the LR.

"Egregiously erroneous, Kemo Sabe" says
Tonto. "Though whereas phemenologically
 speaking, an isolable state of ontological loci
may be taken *prima facie* as coeval with the
sum total of its ostensible appearances, there
may, nonetheless, be obscured, nay, even
ineffable components herein."

The Lone Ranger has been transmogrified too.

Whereas once he was a fair if stern Victorian
    policeman of middle years,
now he is a sort of Southern California
    surfer-kid Highway Patrolman.

"Gosh," says the Lone Ranger, "my Mom and
   Dad sure would be hacked off if there were
any injustice here!"

Thanks a lot, fellas.

Goodbye to everything.

THE LONE RANGER'S JOB SEARCH

The silver mine is running low, and late in life The Lone Ranger applies for a job. The ad reads:

> **WANTED**
> *Masked rider of the plains, capable of returning with us now to those thrilling days of yesteryear, proficiency with exotic, expensive side-arms a must, able to work in a multi-ethnic partnership setting, activist with a strong commitment to truth, justice and the American Way. Must provide own magnificent white stallion w/ insurance. Bi-lingual and computer literate a plus.*

After the interview, the Lone Ranger receives the following letter:

Dear Mr. Ranger:

Thank you for your interest in our organization. Although superbly qualified in your job skills, we regretfully inform you that, after due deliberation, nay, prayerful soul-searching, we have selected from the excellent pool of applicants, someone more exactly suited to our needs as stated in the advertisements and job-description. Thank you again for your interest, and best wishes to you in your puling and pathetic efforts to survive.

Yours truly,

I.M. Ashmuk
I.M. Ashmuk
Exec. Vice President for Personnel
AMERICORP-VERY LTD.

cc: Wotan A. Soul
    Recruitment Director

THE LONE RANGER IN OLD AGE: THREE VIEWS: THIS IS VIEW #1

The Lone Ranger is in his rocker on the porch of the Old Hero's Home.

It is late afternoon, and his one remaining silver Colt is by his side.

He is reading his newspaper as always, when, in *The L.A. Weekly* of Aug. 28. 1987 he happens on the following in an article called "Freudian Freeway" having to do with the then current rash of crazy freeway shootings.

"Coleman perceives an important seductive imagery in the secretness and anonymity of cars and freeways. 'More people are masturbating in cars than on the sofa these days,' he says. "Having a gun and being able to pop people off and fade back into traffic is like being a secret agent. The Lone Ranger, a masked man who was always right and often misunderstood, rides again."

The Lone Ranger experiences a sudden shaking nausea, vertigo, and Cosmic Doubt!

"Was *that* what I was doing? I always acted as an honorable, committed gentleman, trying only to advance the Human Endeavor. I never allied myself with organizations or movements because of their ineptitude and hypocrisy! But this??!!... Me, a sadistic narcissist?!! Was I never a member of the human race I strove to protect??!!" He nearly faints, and is still visibly shaken when

Nurse Titcomb, his unctuous attendant arrives.

"Come along Mr. Ranger, its time to wash up for 'din din'. We're having chipped beef on toast points, and you *know* it's your favorite!"

"Fuck off!" screams the Lone Ranger. "You know I hate 'shit on a shingle', and we have it every goddamn Tuesday!"

"Now, now. Mr. Ranger," says Nurse Titcomb in a voice of syrupy malice, "You promised to behave."

"O very well, goddammit," chokes the Lone Ranger and toddles off to dinner.

THE LONE RANGER IN OLD AGE: THREE VIEWS: THIS IS VIEW #2

He's on the porch reading the newspaper.

Toy replicas, exact ones, of the fabulous silver
  guns are slung over the back of his rocker,
  and
apparently he can't tell the difference.

He reads the same article:

*"The Lone Ranger, the masked man who is
  always right and frequently misunderstood,
  rides again…"*

"Eh." he muses. "They still remember me, see?
  Heh Heh."

Nurse Titcomb, a grim heavyset 'battle-ax' of
  nearly 60 appears.

"All right, Mr. Ranger, it's dinnertime. Let's go.
  Now!"

The Lone Ranger chortles, winks salaciously,
  and croaks:
"You bet, Cutie," and toddles off.

THE LONE RANGER IN OLD AGE.
THREE VIEWS: THIS IS VIEW # 3

The Lone Ranger is sitting in his rocker on the porch of the OH Home. He appears to be reading the newspaper, but actually he is meditating.

The legendary silver chased Colt .45s are in the institution's safe awaiting disposition upon his demise. Yet unbeknownst to anyone, the revolvers are fully loaded with silver bullets that are far in advance of their expiration dates, and the Lone Ranger knows combination to the safe.

The semantic component of his meditation of the moment runs as follows:

"Was I right to do as I did in life? Cannot a case be made that the Lone Ranger was a narcissist, a psychopath, a 'Steppenwolf', an ego-ensnared outsider, a wallflower at the dance of life? I thought not; I tried to live by right thought and action. It was a matter of passion, a personal religion. I was priest in an invisible church of 1. I wonder... But what does it matter? I am at peace."

Nurse Titcomb again. Nurse Titcomb has an additional degree in Social Work. "You know Mr. Ranger, you've been a little distant and inattentive lately. What is it with you? Do you have a problem with women? Do you have 'a woman on your back' as mentioned in the Zen tale? Aren't you a little old for that kind of immaturity?"

"Ah my Dear," says the Lone Ranger in a kindly tone. "If you meet Buddha on the road, kill him."

"What... Mr. Ranger... I fail to see..."

"Come my Dear," smiles the Lone Ranger, "Kindly escort me to dinner."

THE LONE RANGER'S SISTER

Here's the rundown on the Lone Ranger's
   younger sister: Sis Ranger.
A gifted, fabulously beautiful single woman in
   her prime,
   she divides her time amongst three jobs:
neurosurgeon, crusading civil rights attorney,
   and cutting edge rocket scientist.
Her busy schedule has precluded her taking up
   offers for positions
as prima ballerina from the New York State
   Ballet,
   and nose guard from the Green Bay Packers.
A woman of such grit, determination, subtlety
   and decisiveness of mind and strength,
   that all these qualities amply compensate her
   for her petite, size 6 frame.

Once, on a job interview at NASA for the job of
   piloting the first moon rocket
   on history's first round-trip voyage,
The interviewer, (the last man ever to say such
   a thing)
   exclaimed as she opened the door to his
   office:
"But! You're a woman!"
"Right," says Sis Ranger,
"It runs in the family.
So was my mother."

THE LONE RANGER FINDS TRUE LOVE

It happens like the proverbial bolt from the blue, to coin a phrase. One moment he meets her, a week and a half of whirlwind courtship ensues, and right away they're talking marriage. Don't forget, this is one Masked Rider of the Plains now in middle years, eccentric as hell and set in his ways, a curmudgeon and proud of it. So who the hell can he marry? Sadly, it turns out it can't really be Plain Jane Everygirl from Nextdoor, Texas.

So who is this female miracle come to the Lone Ranger after 50,—though he never gave up, never relaxed his standards, and never spoke of it? Why 'tis WONDER-WOMAN, of course! C'mon, you knew it all the time!

Our Boy has never, never met anyone like her, man or woman for that matter. Incredibly erudite, graceful, gracious, witty, warm, committed, brilliant, deeply spiritual, strong, and an athlete, an artist, a teacher and mentor and mother, fair minded and loving, with a physical beauty that would be dazzling by itself were she not so accomplished, and of course: righteously pissed off at men. Never has the Lone Ranger seen someone so decently vulnerable and so truly sophisticated. A renaissance woman to the max.

And it wasn't love at first sight. It was love at about third sight. It took about 3 dates to fire up the engine of "limerance"—the transcendent, high school-era, tender-skyrocket feelings of whole-person-transmuting mystical love to develop,—not just one. Withal, the pervasive feelings the LR is experiencing are: a) this is so blindingly sudden that it's weird, b) that he's known her all his life and this is eternal, calm, cosmic normalcy, and c) that this is like being 15 and giddily in puppy love, while at the same time being 51 and finally knowing what the fuck you're doing, for once.

So there's really not a hell of a lot else to say, which is surprising, because this poem is supposed to be the pinnacle of this collection, the *dénouement*, the climax, the goal of the Lone Ranger's life, toward which all the rest of the events were leading. You know: "*How the Lone Ranger Stopped Being 'Lone' by Finding True Love At Last.*" (C'mon, that's what you were hoping for all along.)

One can only add that the two, the Lone Ranger and the miraculously arrived Wonder Woman are engaged, and planning to be married in love and sanctification, pending the resolution of several important practical issues, like any other 'sane' couple.

One can only add that the Lone Ranger, all of a sudden, for the first time in his life has reason to preserve that life and not risk it so much, a reason to live that is. So he looks both ways before crossing the street twice now instead of just once. He is who he always was of course, but now somehow more intensely and certainly, but he is now less interested in securing justice and more interested in making a life with his beloved. Amen.

Note please that this is not, for once, like the times when the Lone Ranger was a kid and would "fall in love" with a narcissistically projected image of his emotionally withdrawn and punitive mother, not the girl at hand herself and so the whole thing would inevitably fuck up and the LR would get depressed,—so unlike now when the feeling of power, quiet consummate power derives finally and for the first time from *being an adult in love with an adult*. A consummately and cosmically founded/grounded love with his feet finally and firmly planted on the floor of the universe and his head in its skies and his heart beating a sweet intoxicating syrup of thunder. O how he loves her! OOWAH! OOWAH! They are two mountains calmly surveying the distance between them, eternally.

What she has given him is love ontologically, and therefore spiritual connection or grounding etc. etc.—that is to say; he knows that he is no longer expendable. Even though he's always been the Lone Ranger, and let's face it folks, that's not altogether unglamorous. But all that aside, he now *counts* in the universe, and will be able to act accordingly. It is as though his life, black and white all along, has suddenly turned into Technicolor.

THE LONE RANGER'S GREAT LOVE AFFAIR:
THE AFTERMATH
(A Narrative Essay)

The LR'S great love affair has fizzled! That's right: fizzled! Do you know how it feels to be the one and only Masked Rider of the Plains, The Great Sworn Guarantor of Justice for All, Charismatic Folk Hero, and Major Christian Icon to 4 Generations of American Kids, and have your great love affair fizzle? You don't want to know.

Now the causes were typical enough, and indeed the fizzling was by mutual consent. On her side, Wonder Woman objected to the LR's continuingly marginal economic status. His endowment from the silver mine is down to a trickle, and what's more, the price of silver is badly depressed on the ever-receding world market. What with tough times and the shriveled job market, let alone The Closing of the Old West, wherein six-guns and stallions are giving way to helicopters and computers, the Lone Ranger's vocational future is dim indeed. Accordingly, Wonder Woman cannot countenance the continued use of the remaining silver for bullets, when base metals (all right already!—even silver-plated base metals), would do as well. Naturally The Lone Ranger resents this; Our Boy is a Person of Style and Consistency of Image, and will of course retain his silver bullets: hang the expense!

But WW's greater concern in terms of security is even more telling. She is increasingly apprehensive about being mated to an aging cop, credentialed or otherwise. Sooner or later the lightening draw and Zeus like accuracy for shooting guns from hands will fade, (nobody's gettin' any younger ya know),—and some dumb kid seeking a big reputation will like as not eventually render the LR more full of holes than the overpriced Emmenthaler down at the Groovy Cheese Boutique. (Note: It's true that WW is no slouch at evading bullets herself, but, lest she be accused of hypocrisy, remember that *she* uses the deployment of her Magic Bracelets to deflect slugs, and, as this is a Passive Protective System, it is much more dependable over the long haul than is Zen Marksmanship).

So Wonder Woman does not relish being a widow still married to legend, as it were, having too little $$$$ in her old age and, like as not, Tonto as a dependent too. The Lone Ranger is intransigent. He won't give up his racket for a boring if more lucrative job of lesser Social Significance. "I can't give up being a mythic hero," he says. "It's all I know." For his part, the LR needs a little more trust, a bit more respect for who he actually is, and so on. And there's the rub. He figures he has worked long and hard, and suffered much to become the asshole he is by now, and, since these solutions work for him, after a lifetime of floundering grief, he is not about to change. He doesn't feel misunderstood, so much as "non-understood": to wit: "does this broad really know or care about what's important, desperately important to me inside,—that which constitutes who I really, actually am, or does she just see me as good raw material to be re-manufactured by her into a pussy-whipped clone?

Sometime later and still a bachelor, the
Lone Ranger is awarded an
Honorary Doctorate of Being, at the German
Universitat fur
Existenzialismusgewissenschaft
in Alt Heidelberg.
At the commencement, his acceptance speech entitled *"Love: Pro or Con:*
Its Distinguishing Features, Role in the Universe, and Whether It Can Be Recognized and Defined In Time" is delivered to a stock still, packed house. Key excerpts follow:

"Love is the product when two personal histories randomly collide, and the further history created in consequence by the two now interacting, hopefully for the better and not the worse. It exists in time, not in concept."

"There is no automatic 'happily ever-after.' At the inception of a relationship, there is the bedazzled ecstasy of new love, the time of skyrockets and roses, which poets and other nerds are forever on about, what the shrinks call *'limerence'*. Thereafter, the relationship, which is *of this world* and hence imperfect, needs work and maintenance in order to grow. 'One day at a time,' as they say in A.A. This may, repeat *may* get you through over the 'long haul.'"

"Love is 'getting off' when *someone else* hits a

home run. It can become difficult to recognize the Big L even when it stares us in the face, if too much or not enough romance spoils our vision."

"Love is respect for the sanctity of someone else's sentience, subjectivity and separateness, their right to choose: their right to choose wrongly."

"And in concurrence with Martin Buber: The Big L is finally not centrally *about feelings*. It is about *commitment*."

And paraphrasing an anonymous French savant (The Lone Ranger always liked this one): "Love is two people looking outward together toward the same mountain."

"What is love?—
5 feet of heaven in a ponytail."

(Note: O.K. But academic considerations aside, what of the Lone Ranger and Wonder Woman, the couple in question? ed.)

Well, they're still in love, but love *just* ain't the issue! The issue *is feasibility!* Any two people can be in love and/or love one another—who piss one another off or at least just don't get along. Money, style of acculturation, issues of control and respect, one's particular brand of 'nutsiness' automatically pushing the other's 'buttons'—and vice versa, are all obstacles to getting on with it, stuff to work with, if your heart's really in it. So for these two, it's an indeterminate situation.

They still see one another, but the status of the relationship is fluid and changing, the outcome being anybody's guess,—as obtains for most if not all American couples or non-couples, or whatever.

Let's leave them there, to work it out as best they can. Watch this space for updates.

Part the Third

THE QUEST FOR THE MISSING MYSTIC MYTHIC FATHER
or: The Lone Ranger Visits the Old Padre: A Modern Mini-Epic

The Lone Ranger has not had a good week. He is already 45 years old and still without wife, progeny, regular income or recognition from the community. What's more, lately his business has been taking a terrible beating, what with the FBI, the CIA, the Drug Enforcement Administration, the 76th Precinct in Brooklyn, Interpol and the Hill Street Blues rounding up so many Bad Guys that there are no longer enough to go around.[1] On top of this, he feels he has all but blown it with his latest heartthrob, an up-and-coming, hot-shit lady lawyer from New Hampshire. Recently he has applied to the Foreign Legion, only to be told by a certain Capt. Montaigne: "Merci bien Monsieur 'Ronjay,' but we of the Legion do not even consider 45 year old masked idealists."

At very least, the Lone Ranger needs a vacation. He decides to visit his old mentor, the Old Padre. Now only a few people know the true identity of the Lone Ranger: the Old Padre; his nephew Dan Reid; Old Jim Blaine, an ex-Ranger and sometime mentor of the LR, full partner in the LR's silver mine which he runs, and who makes his silver bullets, and is therefore aka the "Old Miner"; Tonto of course; the late

---

1- The LAPD is not included here, as apparently they got a garbled version of the message. Back then they seemed to perceive "bust bad guys" as "beat black guys."

Grandma Frisbee and the author of the current piece, but of course I'll never tell.

We join him now at his office on L.A.'s Sunset Strip as he prepares to leave on his trip. With the hard times, the office has grown seedy, and the silver letter-decals on the window of the one-room, two-desk storefront are peeling. Still legible however, they read:

RANGER and TONTO
Do—Gooders
A Limited Partnership
Charismatics a Specialty

Tonto is seated at his desk when the LR enters and says: "Tonto. I need a break. I gotta beat it for a spell. To paraphrase Rodney Crowell in "Leavin' Louisiana in the Broad Daylight"

"Kemo Sabe gotta go
Gotta get outa here
Gotta get outa town
I'm tired o' hangin' around
Gotta roll on
Between the ditches."

"Unhhhhh," says Tonto, "Where you go, Kemo Sabe?"

"Gonna see the Padre, Ace, talk it over, kick

back, re-group, take cosmic inventory, so to speak. Two weeks. Take my calls, willya Buddy?"

"But" says Tonto, "What about the big coke bust comin' up, and remember the tax boys wanna see our books."

LR: I have spoken, Tovarich. Special pleading. I'm outta here!
T: OK Baby. (sighs) Have a good one. Zei gesund, go in health.
LR: Farewell, Kemo Sabe. (and leaves through the back door).

"Jesus," thinks Tonto, "what I gotta go through in this outfit!"—but nonetheless props his moccasins up on his desk and resumes his reading, a monograph entitled:

"An Inquiry into the Ontology of Sociopathic Behavior and Ideation with Implications for Social Policy, especially Walrus Poaching: as Cuisine, and as Felony"

This last was written by his friend Ook Lewk Ook Pik, an Eskimo exchange student he knew in his days in the Social Ethics Dept. at Balliol College, Oxford.

Now the LR is in the backyard preparing for his trip. First, he re-adjusts Silver's shoes, saddle and other tack. No hot pursuits this time, no headin' 'em off at the pass, no hell-for-leather anything: he wants gear for a leisurely cross-country schlep,—fewer oats to the mile,—you know what I mean? Next, he applies an innocuous liquid compound of Kiwi Cordovan Shoe Polish, orange vegetable dye, and solvent to the shimmering white coat of the magnificent stallion, the purpose being to disguise him as a sorrel.

"Say wot?!" says the Great Horse, shying a little as the Lone Ranger begins.

"Sorry Big Fella, but this time we're riding incognito."

"Jesus" says Silver, "What I gotta go through in this outfit! If I were human, I'd need a drink."

The Lone Ranger, no one to screw around with these days, counters by singing:

"Who's sorrel now?"

Who's sorrel now?

Who's heart is aching and breaking each vow?"

"All right, all right!" says Silver, "Just get it done!"

It is done.

Next, The LR doffs his mask (!), white Stetson 10 gallon, and the rest of his LR outfit, the campy white jeans and tunic-like shirt, and dons in their stead some plain brown cotton-knit jeans and a "normal" 2 pocket western style sport shirt, brown boots and a conservative brown 5 gallon Stetson, like that of a Texas oil-person, or say, LBJ. He applies a false mustache: your regular western tourist out for a leisurely schlep to a resort area. Of course, the handsomely silver-chased match-grade Colt revolvers and the attendant firmament of silver bullets are dead giveaways, and as such are forsworn and put in a safe in the backyard garage. In their place a small and lethal Israeli made sub-machine gun is carefully concealed in a fake champagne magnum, and that in turn is placed for easy access in the right-hand American Tourister saddlebag. Transformed, the Lone Ranger mounts and sets off. Under his breath he mutters: HI- YO Sil— uh, Brownie, Awayyyyyyy......."

"Jesus" thinks Silver, "Here we go again, only boy: this one is 'heavy!'" And the Lone Ranger rides again, but this time *not* like the wind.

Here begins the leisurely and so far uneventful schlep outbound along the side of the San Bernardino Freeway. The Old Mission where the Old Padre stays is in the general area of Big Bear and Lake Arrowhead, though of course I can't tell you exactly where. There, the road winds around and around and around up the mountain if you are ascending, and around and around and around down the mountain if you are descending.

Such is the nature of travel, and such is the nature of language. Such is the nature of the road, and such is the nature of the mountain. Remember this, Dear Reader.

And it is nightfall of the third day when the Lone Ranger astride the brown Silver reaches the base of the Right Mountain. It will be one full day's ride to the top, to the Mission. And here begins the Lone Ranger's Dark Night of the Soul. The very second Silver's front hoof touches the trail, lightening flashes crack and dazzle the sky, thunder cannonades the heavens and the earth, the wind comes on like a frigid whistling scythe, and the rain and cold come down like hell. There is no place off the skinny, precipitous trail to shelter, no equipment for it, and no turning back. The Lone Ranger and Silver slog on soaked to the skin and cold to the bone. It is autumn and the rain gives way to snow in blizzard assault that blinds the eyes of horse and man, and icy winds that razor—slice at the flesh, and still they slowly, blindly slog on in rising pain and suffering. And then hail which stings the body like birdshot, and it is winter. And abruptly it stops, only to be replaced by a hot and searing night wind, a sirocco, an arid Santa Ana that parches the skin and deranges the mind. Mad, they slog on. And the moon changes abruptly and quickly through all its shapes, like a speeded up movie: no moon, sliver of moon, crescent moon, quarter moon, half moon, gibbous moon, full moon. And the full moon holds: still. Cessation. Calm.

And there are light winds. And clouds come and hide the moon. And there are shots! That's right. Shots!—blasting in the middle distance and the bullets spitting and twitting through the leaves by the side of the road and slugged into the dirt around them. And the Lone Ranger hunching low and that horse are off the road like a *rocket* and into a defile by the opposite side of the road and almost behind a boulder in a twinkling, and that Uzi, always on a string to the saddle horn is out of its spring-loaded fake champagne bottle in a sliced second and a bullet comes and grazes the boulder and a rock fragment comes and smashes into the nose of the Lone Ranger bloodying it and the ricocheting bullet comes and creases his left shoulder. And the horse and he are kneeling down now, covered. And there is nothing see; it is pitch-tar black, and there are no muzzle flashes and nothing to shoot at, and he dare not move, and he is pinned down and they may have night scopes. And the deadly, incessant barrage continues hour after hour and the full moon, still cloud covered, is lowering in the vault of the sky, down beside the other side of the road.

Will this be the end? His life flashes before him. His auspicious birth and stultified boyhood in an eastern big city, his elaborate education at fine schools, his coming west to find freedom and a sense of his own strength, his joining of the Texas Rangers and the massacre too soon thereafter which only he survived, his blood brotherhood with the Indian Tonto who saved his life, the solemn oath of anonymity he took in order to preserve the Right,—whereby he became the Lone Ranger, and, with a surging power greater than all of these, the flooding sense of his lifetime alienation and desolating loneliness.

Wounded, disconsolate about his life, grimly doubtful of its meaning, and now it seems he is about to be extinguished by random madness before anything can be reconciled. *De profundis*: this is the ultimate agony. Must it end like this, at the beginning of his quest? Must it end like this, life having always been bleak? Must it end like this, pre-empting any glimmer of hope there may be in this crisis, by whatever strange, random luck there is?

Will this be the end? Here in this black nothingness, indeterminate, intermediate, in the middle of his urgent life with nothing decided, at the very initiation of his pilgrimage of mid-life? Death in "the middle of the parenthesis" as it were,—by loss of blood, exposure, starvation or murder by the Anonymous? For hours, the suffering, the doubt, the unknowingness. The sense of betrayal by God or a bad shake from the universe: to be pitched into darkness eternal, having never known light? No! No! In utter despair, the Lone Ranger's mind goes dark for 100 years.

And a miracle happens. The clouds disappear from the face of the moon now almost set by the other side of the road, and—because when the moon sets, they will come to get him—the Lone Ranger in last desperation throws a small stone to earth 10 yards to his right and screams as it lands and at the same time peeks out around the boulder as all of the fire is drawn toward the impacting stone and they are there silhouetted against the moon and its light, horsemen, 4 of them, dismounted, in strange capes and weird, tall, conical hats with silver, runic figurations, with a terrible array of weapons all ranged along the other side of the road and in that instant the Uzi speaks and scans and there is the terrible joint racket of the chopper and the dim thud of the 9mm. slugs hitting skulls and torsos and shocked grunts and the flickering sight of the bodies punched back over the precipice and one falling scream for 1,000 feet and their horses scattering and falling off and then one voice moaning several feet below the road and the moaning abruptly stops, and it is over.

There is nothing for it; it is still pitch dark. He will never know who they were, and he knows that. Wounded, adrenalized, disgusted and after vomiting copiously, the Lone Ranger mounts and wends on. He has never killed anybody before, except for his brother the lawyer, who, being a yuppie, deserved it.

Bleeding, in shock, and exhausted beyond madness, he plods on. There is no word for this kind of fatigue. Some miles of riding like the dead. The first glimmer of first light. It is almost spring.

Incredibly, a very old couple, backpacking, is walking down the trail as he slowly ascends. They both wear old and tattered uniforms of the California Highway Patrol.

"Hi Sonny," says the woman, carefully looking him over, seeing the mad eyes, the bleeding nose and the torn shoulder. "Have you had some hard luck?"

"Hello Ma'am and Sir" says the Lone Ranger. It is reflex arcs only talking now. "Yes, it's been a tough night." Silver whinnies slightly but threateningly.

"What about those wounds. Son?" the old woman says.

"A falling rock, Ma'am."

"Son," says the old man, "We used to be with the Highway Patrol, and I ought' a know a bullet wound when I see one. You better come with us."

"A falling rock. Sir," says the Lone Ranger, looking 1,000 miles through the old man's head.

Something in the dead glare of the Lone Ranger's glazed eyes gives the old man to know that this mysterious, mad, yet somehow controlled person in the bedraggled tourist clothes is the greatest highway patrolman of all time himself, and not under any circumstances to trifle with him.

"O.K. Son," says the old woman, "we have a first aid kit here with us here, climb on down and let me have a look at those woun... uh, injuries."

"Yes, thank you," he says dazedly and does so, and the wounds are cleaned and bandaged.

He remounts slowly.

"Well" the old folks say, "Good luck. Sonny."

"Thank you," says the Lone Ranger, "and God bless you."

He rides slowly off, unable even to look at them. They walk slowly down the trail.

"Strange fella', Maud" the old man says. "Yes Harry, but good somehow, and compelling."

Another hour and a quarter and the Lone Ranger rounds the final curve in the path, and there at last, in its little clearing in the woods, stands the Old Mission, just beginning to glow with the first real rays of sunlight. It is spring, and it is dawn. With leaden feeling, the Lone Ranger dismounts, tethers Silver, and approaches the small, stucco, old-style California mission, surmounted by a cross just beginning to cast a shadow. The Old Padre lives here, alone. The LR knocks on the door.

A tired, old, Spanish inflected voice answers: "Who ees it?"

"It is I, Padre mio. John Reid."

(John Reid is the Lone Ranger's real name.)

"One momento, my son."

The door opens to reveal the Old Padre. Slight of stature, stooped with age, the kindly, lined face topped by a monkish tonsure: a fringe of grey hair around the crown of his bald, age-spotted head. He is wearing a loud Hawaiian floral print shirt—crucifix hanging in front, balloon like cotton pants with purple thong sandals, and in one hand holds the remains of a can of Lone Star Beer. The Lone Ranger can see the TV through the door, and the OP had been watching the gorgeous Elvira slink around the screen on her Saturday morning Grade C horror-movie show.

"How ees it with you my son?"
"But Padre..."
"Come een, my son."

The Lone Ranger enters and begins to speak. The words rush forth. "Padre nothing is working I feel so..."

"Peace, my son. You are injured and tired. You must rest. We will talk tomorrow. Come, my son. We will have some wine."

They drink wine as the dawn rises and the last flames and embers wink out in the fireplace in the old room, glowing now both from the incipient dawn and a little from the dying fire, and at length the OP leads the LR to a bed in an adjoining room. The Lone Ranger sleeps for 24 hours. He has a great dream which lasts the length of his sleep. He dreams of the featureless black expanse of a giant unlit movie screen, upon which there is nothing. Nothing, nothing ever, nothing for the length of the dream, nothing for the duration of the universe. Nothing.

He awakens spent, only to see the OP in the doorway beckoning him to breakfast. When the bacon and grits are gone, and the second coffees drunk, and when the smoke from the cigarettes has wafted away, the OP says: "Come my son, we will work in the garden."

There, amid the growing things, the food plants, commences the Lone Ranger's last great instruction from the Old Padre. Bending to water some new corn, the Padre begins:

"What is troubling you, my son?"

"I have lost my way. Padre mio. In the world what is there for a man?"

"There is love and work, my son. That is all there is. So said Dr. Freud."

"But Father, I can find neither. I am alone and doubt the value of my work."

"Work is whatever you conceive it to be John, whatever calls you, regardless of what the world may say, and love is only the joining of complimentary histories by two people. Women are us, yet mysteriously different, even as we are them, yet ineffable in part to them."

"But Padre, I do not feel a man, I have found neither."

"You were already a man, my son, when you came here to seek me."

"But Padre, I have looked to you so. You have found peace in your pastoral work and in your love of God."

"I am only a man, my son. An old man who loves his beer. The secret is to take your mother and your father into yourself, to become your own parents, to give yourself the gift of your mother's unconditional love, and your father's demanding love. This is to be as you are, were always, and always will be. This is to make you legitimate to yourself. It is as Dr. Frohm says. And then love comes of its own accord when you are upright and ready, complete and sufficient unto yourself, re-made by yourself you're your experience, needing nothing."

"Padre. Padre."

"Call me Jose, my son. You know me now, and later you will come to know your mother."

"Padre...Jose, I begin to see."

"Come with me, my son." He leads the Lone Ranger behind a fence to a wooded field behind the mission. There, to the astonishment of the Lone Ranger, arrayed on a picnic table, is a duplicate Lone Ranger outfit, only finer than any he has ever owned, and two silver automatic pistols, sleek, more accurate, and more modern with their 14 shot capacity firepower than his legendary heirloom Colt six-shooters back in L.A.

"Let us shoot, my son," says OP. On a stone fence in the middle distance, 24 bottles are standing.

"I will go first, John." It was the Old Padre who taught the Lone Ranger how to shoot.

Taking one of the pistols, the OP blazes away with surprising speed, and 11 bottles in a row fall. He misses the 12th.

"You never missed before, my father Jose."

"I am old, John. Please shoot now. Be careful, that pistol throws low and a little to the left."

Now the Lone Ranger fires away with the strange yet impossibly familiar automatic. The first 11 fall consecutively in a flash; he misses the 12th.

"Good shooting, my son!"

"Ten was the best I ever did before. Padre." There is a pause. "That's the spirit, my son. I can tell you no more. I can teach you no more of the craft of life. I will not see you again. Go now, and prosper. Go now. Goodbye, my son."

"Yes, I understand. Thank you. Goodbye, Padre mio."

They embrace wordlessly. And now the Lone Ranger turns.

And now the Lone Ranger dons his new outfit and straps on the automatics. After all, it is a new day. Taking Silver out by the barn, he prepares to hose down the great stallion to restore his true color.

"Er, what's that Lone?" the great horse asks.

"Just a hose. Big Fella, to get rid of that sorrel gunk."

"Jesus. Cowboy, it's about time. Say, let me lay a little tune on you," and Silver sings: "Hose sorry now? Hose sorry now? Hose heart is aching and breaking each vow?"

"All right. Silver. I deserved that."

"Jesus." thinks Silver. "I'm glad that's over with!"

After drying his mount, the Lone Ranger sets off. He has arranged for the Old Padre to burn his tourist outfit, and to donate the sub-machine gun to the Salvation Army or some other nice army who can use it.

Thus begins the Lone Ranger's down-going to the World. Crooning "I was so much older then, I'm younger than that now", he walks Silver slowly down the mountain. Half way down, rounding the curved flank of the mountain, the Lone Ranger sees the ocean-sea far below. Gazing rapt at the ocean, he stops. Gradually yet powerfully, lastingly, he begins to feel different. Quiet and strong. Consummately caring yet utterly heedless. It is a slow, strong, sure yet apocalyptic change of consciousness, the epiphany of the self, yet the dissolving of the ego. He stares deep into the sea, high up at the mountain and, one with the sea and the sky and the mountain, the forest and all of life and love or almost so, he pauses for a moment, draws a deep breath and then spurs Silver to a full gallop shouting the primeval "HI YO SILVER AWAYYYYY!" And rides streaking down the mountain toward the World, this time once again, like the wind.

THE LONE RANGER AT THE MOMENT OF DEATH

- goodbye,
it was nice knowing you,
thank you all very much.
- teach love. -
(the faint thud of hoof beats receding)
white light
- Hi—Yo—Silver!
AWAAAAAAAYYYYYY......
and fade to black,
so far as anyone knows

THE LONE RANGER ON SUPERMAN'S FLIGHT
or:
THE LONE RANGER AS SCIENTIST

In retirement now, the Lone Ranger has taken to writing learned monographs on a variety of topics, to occupy his mind in a time when his normal activities of wrong-righting and justice-procurement in the Old West have dwindled to practically nothing. In one such, entitled "Superman and the Myth of Flight", he writes:

> Superman cannot fly! Yes, that's what I said, Superman cannot fly! I base this seemingly astonishing assertion on two broad areas of contention: one an analysis of the physics and phenomenology of the situation, the other being anecdotal.
>
> In the first place, when Superman is seen apparently flying through the air, there seems no evidence of any cause of sustained or powered flight. What propels him? Apparently nothing! Surely he isn't using a hidden engine, not given his widely known candor. And while he can leap tall buildings at a single bound all right, his "flying"—if merely super-long jumps, would surely succumb to gravity sooner or later, and accordingly exhibit a parabolic character.
>
> Superman or not, the dude is not immune to the physical laws of the universe; "Supernaturalman" he ain't. Yet he gives the impression of sustained level

flight. The answer must lie elsewhere, perhaps in something like the following:

Unlike myself, a regular guy traveling incognito, the dude is from another planet, so he probably has a different cell structure, a fundamentally different protoplasm chemistry[1] -the molecular components of which he can magnetize or de-magnetize at will, attracting or repelling the earth and other objects, and so create the appearance of flight. But this isn't true flight; it's a form of levitation, although I admit this is rather a semantic point.

The other argument is that I know Superman, and he told me (secretly, of course)—that "something like this was the case."

Ed. Note: Some critical opinion holds that the logic displayed here is specious, the fruit of the senescent Lone Ranger's thinly disguised professional jealousy of Superman, the only other superhero anywhere near his stature. Additionally, a number of respected critics hold that the provenance or authenticity of this fragment, ostensibly from the LR's later writings, is at best dubious.

---

[1]—*"The man of steel"*—*does that tell you something?* -

DAN REID

I think it is significant
That the Lone Ranger *did* bare his face
To one woman,
Albeit a dying woman.

What happened was this:

Prologue: The Lone Ranger and Tonto arrive in the immediate aftermath of an Indian massacre of the wagon-train bearing the LR's sister-in-law Linda, (that lovely lady from Virginia) and her infant son, nephew to the LR. The Masked Rider and his Faithful Indian Companion come upon an abandoned trunk in the wreckage which bears an engraved plate inscribed with the name Linda Reid. As has long been known to legend, the mother and her son were on their way to join her husband, the boy's natural father: the Lone Ranger's big brother: Capt. Dan Reid Sr., late of the Texas Rangers, and now lamentably late altogether.

FLASH FORWARD

About 14 years hence, the Lone Ranger and Tonto somehow get wind that the Lone Ranger's lost nephew, now approaching young manhood, is being raised by a benevolent old lady (Grandma Frisbee – then a younger woman) as her step-grandson, since she rescued him from the site of the aforementioned massacre which took the life of his mother, and of which he,—the infant later to be named Dan Reid Jr.- was the sole survivor, —said rescue taking place shortly before the

LR and T arrived on-scene. Now, upon finally learning the story, the LR and T head forthwith for that ever-popular, (and highly specific) tourist Mecca: The North Country.

They arrive to confront a dying Grandma Frisbee!

From her deathbed she says:

"And who are you sir, to burst in upon the privacy of a dying old woman, armed, in the company of a Red Indian no less, and wearing a black mask, at that?!!"

"I am the rightful paternal uncle of the boy you are raising, Grandma Frisbee, and I have come for him now. The mask is part of a vow I have made, these guns are for the saving of life, not the taking of it, and as for the Indian, he is my brother."

"And how, young man," says Grandma Frisbees. "May I be assured that you are telling the truth? Can you identify this?"

Now Grandma Frisbee with what is to be her last movement removes from her bosom a wedding locket, the open halves of which display the inward facing portraits of a married couple, the boy's mother Linda, and her husband—the Lone Ranger's older brother, Capt. Dan Reid Sr., himself killed by yet *another* vile ambush, that earlier one at the hands of the fiendish Butch Cavendish and his gang. Under the locket's portraits are engraved the names Daniel and Linda.

"Yes ma'am," says the Lone Ranger pointing to one leaf of the locket, "this man was my brother" and turning to his nephew, "Your father Dan Reid Sr."

The old woman ponders the portraits for long minutes before her face softens and she says: "Yes, take him; he is your blood. I named him Daniel after the portrait in the locket. You must vow to raise him as your own."

"Yes ma'am, I do so vow," says the Lone Ranger.

There is a pause.

"Sir," says Grandma Frisby, "Might I see your face that I may die in confidence before you go off with my grandson?"

"Why certainly, Ma'am," responds the Lone Ranger without the slightest hesitation, and facing Grandma Frisbee, the Lone Ranger doffs his mask. Grandma Frisbee gazes at him for a long beat, averts her glance for a moment to the young countenance of Dan Reid, then back to the Lone Ranger for a second, smiles weakly but beatifically, and closes her eyes for the last time.

"GRANDMA FRISBEE!"—suddenly expostulates the agitated and now twice abandoned child Dan Reid.

And the Lone Ranger quietly intones "Softly now Dan! She can't hear you any longer! She's sleeping now..."

Now the poignant tableau freezes as the three stand around the bed, heads downcast. At the foot of the bed, hat in hand, stands the barefaced Lone Ranger, gazing down upon the quiet visage of Grandma Frisbee in repose. We of course, are standing in back of him, that is to say our POV is from in back of the Lone Ranger, and *we* do not get to see his face.

Thus began the tenure of Daniel Reid Jr., under the stewardship of his uncle, the Lone Ranger.

THE LONE RANGER AND HIS MOTHER: THE RECONCILIATION

Hard is the fortune of all womankind.
She's always constrained; she's always confined.
Constrained by her father until she's a wife,
Confined by her husband the rest of her life.
      Old Anglo-American Folk Song

Who are these women? What do they want?
      Sigmund Freud

While searching for clues in a musty old attic in the North Country, the Lone Ranger comes upon the dusty manuscript of an early draft of a fine poem:

AMALIA FREUD TO HER SON SIGMUND
By Ioanna Warwick

(Pressed for time, the Lone Ranger browses the following excerpts:)

My golden Sigi, those cigars
will be the death of you.
You have it after me, that passion, that excess
spiraling from a vase like a summer bouquet,
an anarchy of desire
that must be talked into lying down.
Did you know in my youth I was thought
a great beauty?
A man, not your father,
said to me once,
"One could fall into your eyes
and keep falling—"
But I don't blame you if you never

saw me as Amalia.
To a child his mother is only his mother...

...You say you don't understand women.
A woman is a mother.
It's the most terrifying
thing in the world I know.
You laugh that I pace
like a caged lioness,
running to the landing, the door,
for an hour before you are to visit.
I tried to explain to a childless friend:
"It's the same as what you feel
for a lover—except more. ...

...somewhere you wrote
how important it is for a man
to have been his mother's favorite son:
it gives him a life-long
feeling of triumph.
That is enough for me.
Remember your gloves and scarf:
it's so easy to catch cold...

When the Lone Ranger is not working,
dreaming, thinking
or otherwise engaged—
that is: in such reflective moments as he has -
the pain of his mother
shrieks behind his cortex.

But now, as the Lone Ranger finishes reading,
behind his misted eyes, a Great Reverie develops.

Flashback

The Lone Ranger remembers
in glimpses of
the long, long ago
when, of a random afternoon
in the dread dreamtime
of the Second World War
his young mother took him to a movie—
the Astor, one known then as an "art" theater
where films of a more serious intent,
European films, were shown.
A theater of restrained décor,
maroon and wood, more an *atelier*
so unlike the gaudy
Arabian fantasy
"seraglios" and *"palaces"*
of the popular theaters.

A boy of only 5 or 6 then,
he remembers seeing only great faces
very close-up on the screen—
sepia brown that long ago,
a foreign language spoken,
ghostly writing changing on the bottom of the screen,
runic to the child,
a man's face and a woman's,
sad and tender
in expressions of love
denied, betrayed or impossible
and although the Lone Ranger could not
    fathom this,
his mother's silent crying.
How could the Lone Ranger,
as a little boy
understand the private sorrow
of his mother, the little girl?

Flashback
(Mis en scène)

With her husband, The Lone Ranger's Father,
the screaming, the shrieking
the caustic contumely
of mutual blame
for betrayal
never stopped:
the hopes of each of them
in the other and for both:
she to become
a liberated princess
in the great metropolis,
he a man of stature
power and money
a "knight" in the ruling establishment—
these dreams
dashed forever
by the Lone Ranger's
crashing the party
with his birth:
they, always and ever
unprepared for him,
children having children
their campaigns
sidetracked now
forever

Flashback

Curfew is at 12:00 midnight
For her first date at age 18
the event
probably long delayed

even for those mid—1930's
but they arrive home a couple of minutes before.
Framed in the doorway
is Max!
her father
The Lone Ranger's grandfather to be

Max:
standing there
in his sleeve garters
arm akimbo
fists on his hips
turn of the century National Guardsman
Republican
sometime private detective,
boxer
now and forever
the stern Victorian storekeeper,
and hard, unremitting moralist.

He will work 47 years, never missing a day,
in his 3 piece suit,
worn also on Sunday,
his one-day off,
and later
steadfastly
in retirement too.

Max:
ominously waiting now
his face like something quarried
he is
waiting for the midnight clock
to strike infraction
waiting

for his daughter
to blow her Cinderella deadline
so he can turn her into a pumpkin
which he does anyway in the frightened eyes
of those stunned youths:
catastrophic shame for her
terror for her credulous young man.

Thus the message stamped on her:

The world is terrifying, overwhelming,
I struggle in it with discipline for all of us,
and I represent it.
As you are born
a woman child
you are inherently flawed.
You are partial, only partial
and you are, by your gender
not among the sane.
You are dithering, vulnerable, incompetent and weak
Thus for you -
—though women have their place -
the world is a dangerous country,
do not go there.

This message to women
ceaselessly replayed
to her
by the world
is sung into the bones of the sons.

Thus it is relayed into
The Lone Ranger's earliest days
stated and implied
and daily thereafter:

You are beautiful Darling,
And intelligent,
but fragile,
flawed in strength.
Throughout you
runs a hairline crack
and were you to play
football
with the tough kids
up the block,
you would shatter
in an instant.
You are perforce "the boy in the bubble"
and therefore, on your very life
you may not stray from Mommy's tit.
So stay an infant
never a voter
and never enfranchised
as human.
I do not know you
but you may never leave me.
For you as for me
the world is a dangerous country:
do not go there
but you are innocent of even this.
Kept by me
from dangerous knowledges,
- your knowing itself is damaged -
this extortion of consciousness
now autonomous
replenishing itself
in endless circle.

Hobbled so, you cannot navigate
the world.
From duty then
I must kill you as a man
so that you will be safe.

She does not know this
as revenge
nor will she ever.
But thus, by magical dark fiat of the mother,
the son is to remain a perpetual infant
and obversely
the son is to become The Lone Ranger.

Nothing was ever right.
Nothing was ever safe.
Screaming, nagging
red words, black looks
a life of dissatisfaction
a life of ceaseless accusation
indictments
blame, blame, blame
followed in cycle
by guilt, guilt, guilt
at her own excesses:
- *I didn't mean it*
I didn't mean it-

Intrusiveness
phone call surveillance
mail summarily opened and inspected
coupled with her husband's
barging without knocking
through the door
into the exquisitely sensitive
adolescent's room

and always,
always shouting toward him
how, due to his relentless malfeasance
whether from evil or madness or both,
he was, via continuing aggravation:
killing her.

Flashback

Once when he was a youth
going on young man,
the Lone Ranger's Mom
driven to hysterical
weeping screaming rage
--by what offense
fancied or actual
no longer remembered -
(it was always the same) -
she crazily attacked him
with a coat hanger
battering him harmlessly
about the forearms.

The hanger
was clad
in padded pink silk
and dedicated to the closet storage
of her mink coat,
that consummately vindicating
women's treasure of the day,
yet far too little
of what was owed her
by world and love

The hanger raised like a saber
she came screaming
lurching to the attack
her shapeless housecoat
luffing like a sail in a crosswind
her face an arpeggio
of morphing grimaces
irrigated by hot squalls of tears

harmlessly and easily
The Lone Ranger disarmed his mother
taking away the hanger
dissolving her aggression
in an instant
and leaving her there to stand
weeping for all
that had ever been lost.

In that instant of epiphany
he first saw her:
a little girl,
weeping, weeping,
her doll forcibly
torn away.

Flashback

The Lone Ranger
between roads unseen
utterly effaced
in the windowless
vault of depression
world featureless now
the very air
vapor of lead

and immune to language
but the iron *mandamus*
of self-loathing.

A young man
made of wood
shipped from place to place
when bodily mobile at all
unable to think
unable to be
needing a warm coat.

Shopping
his mother
selects a parka
massive-thick boxy grey
with squares of faint blue lines
as overlay —
a shapeless nondescript
near shroud-like thing.

Only very dimly aware
he doesn't like it
he has no strength
no will
to know it out loud
or say it,
he numbly assents,
no energy to afford
for a forthright decision
only:
the pain, the pain:
get me out of here
take me home
let me go to sleep.

she says:
"it will keep you warm"

and The Lone Ranger will never forget
his mother's face
that cold sharp Brooklyn winter morning
drum-skin tight
seemingly flat stretched
pancake make-up in the sun
eyes shining,
confusion in stop motion

mounting terror of the unknown -
that it may be inexorable
and deadly
hence
dread of
the devastation of the future,
of universal, everlasting
ruin

and burgeoning anguish for
her incomprehensibly broken son
her love impacted,
neutralized
in frantic yearning
to be able to save her child
to repair him.

Flash Forward

Long years later
in widowhood
living with another son,
she dies very old.

secure with children and grandchildren
without struggle
without responsibility
progressively demented
but relaxed and charming now
she has had, thank God
a few years' happiness,
a few years' peace.

By luck
or from the suasion of
whatever occult force
the LR calls his mother
days before the onset
of the affliction
which soon will end her life
and therewith begins to reconcile
the great pain laden grievance
of their lives.
This, not having spoken in 5 years:
nor to his brother as well.
5 years estranged "radio silence"
at an end.

When she turns gravely worse
The Lone Ranger flies there
and bedside
as she is dying
grips her hand

saying to her:
"I love you.
Thank you.
My brother and I are reconciled..."
She appears to turn her head toward him -
a miniscule movement nearly invisible
her lips opening less than a centimeter
attempts to speak.
- The Lone Ranger believes she understands -
"Don't try to talk, Ma.
Don't try to talk..."

Orphaned now
whatever his age,
after a time
The Lone Ranger finds
that there is a hole in the air
through which, oddly enough
all he can see
is the benign and gentle, innocent little girl
underneath it all -
a gentle flower born
who never understood the weather
and so could only shriek.

Yes, now something vague but huge
is missing—
pervasive,
like a tincture in the water
or a faint discoloration, cooling
or hollowing
of the air
and yet...
and yet...

AHH— THE HELL WITH IT!
NO MORE, NO MORE!
She did what she could
against terrible odds
of benightedness
and pain -

Now
The Lone Ranger stands,
looks up, breathes deeply
and abruptly
flings the hot coal
burning in his naked hand
for 60 some odd years
flings it arcing high
and away over the endless sea
and at the apex of its climb
twin blurs of silver in the lower air
as the lightning revolvers
flash up from his hips
to blast the glowing coal
into a slow shower
of ephemeral crimson stars
falling stately now
to the surface
of the world's wide ocean sea,
hissing to extinction

Part the Fourth

**EPILOG:
THE LONE RANGER RETURNS
TO NORMANDY,
50 YEARS LATER TO THE DAY,
THAT IS: JUNE, 6 1994.**

The LR returns alone, unnoticed,
to Normandy, 50 years later to the day,
in civilian sport clothes,
but with a baseball cap
indicating his old unit
and his jacket bespattered with the medals
won for his part
in the invasion
to destroy history's consummate monstrosity.
And yes, by deadly force of arms, that time.

For once he wears no mask,
and is faceless amongst
his brother old and long gray vets,
which is mask enough this day.

The President, a young man not born then
and not a bad speechmaker,
says quite simply
that with their comrades in arms
when they were young
the Boys of Normandy
saved the world,
and that we shall carry that progress forward
we, the children of their sacrifice -
and how self-empowered free persons from
   democracies
can always lick those afflicted with totalitarian
   discipline.

Wreaths are laid
anthems played and sung
planes flown by
saluting guns discharged
historians consulted briefly on camera.

Today's generals
and some common soldiers
of D-Day,—average old guys and the greatest
    heroes ever of the world speak.
The vast, uncommon carnage remembered
the ceaselessly cruel memories of loss of buddies
this among tears shed here under a woman's hat
and there beneath the visor of a cap with
    airborne insignia,
over the creased face of an old man,
nearby the stretching acres
of white marble crosses and stars.

At other cemeteries
Kraut and G.I. veterans interact
perhaps in some forgiveness
but at least in mutual grief
and the anguished respect of one blooded soldier
    for another

Can there be a future?
The Lone Ranger walks away.

Never, never forget!

The Lone Ranger walks away
alone

Steve Goldman

Steve Goldman was the founder/MC of The Venice Poetry Readings at The New Library, at the Venice, CA branch of the Los Angeles Public Library. His poems and articles have appeared in a variety of publications, including *Solo, Verve, Glue, The Venice Beachhead, The Santa Monica Bay News, Abalone Moon, Poetry International, poeticdiversity,* and *The Walt Whitman Pioneer.*

He is the author of four chapbooks, *The George Winston Poems, To Love and Back, Middleweight Zen,* and *Rachmunas,* the latter having been selected for publication, and another full-sized poetry collection, *The Unplanned Child,* forthcoming - which won an Honorable Mention from Cedar Hill Press of Cleveland. He is an associate editor of the online poetry magazine *Abalone Moon,* and was a co-editor of *The Great American Poetry Show,* an annual magazine in bound book form. He was nominated for a Pushcart Prize for a poem in this book, *The Birth of the Lone Ranger.* He is a fencing instructor specializing in the teaching of children, and is the founder/director and chief instructor of The Venice Fencer's club, a *salle d'armes* in Venice, CA, under Maitre de Armes Loc The Nguyen. He is the founder/director of *Daybreak,* an ethno-music chorus.

He holds, with Octavio Paz, that we have lost our poetic sense, and with it our humanity, and his efforts are aimed at re-infusing American culture with the one, and hence the other.

About This Edition

This revised edition of **The Canon of the Lone Ranger** was assembled from a variety of files and proofed by RD Armstrong. The book was then laid out by Chris Yeseta.

For details and/or quotes, please contact poetraindog@gmail.com or visit either of these two websites: www.lummoxpress.com (RD Armstrong) or http://yazoota.tripod.com/ (Chris Yeseta)

www.ingramcontent.com/pod-product-compliance
Lightning Source LLC
Chambersburg PA
CBHW071235090426
42736CB00014B/3095